P9-CJY-146

man
speaks
dog

by Donald Morris and Kimberly Zuidema

Design: Kimberly Zuidema
Editor: Andrea Donner

Printed in Canada

Aidi
Akbash
Alapaha Blueblood Bulldog
Alaskan Klee Kai
American Bulldog
American Hairless Terrier
American Pit Bull Terrier
Anatolian Shepherd
Anglo-FranÁais
Appenzeller Mountain Dog
Ariégeois
Argentino Dogo
Australian Kelpie
Austrian Pinscher
Azawakh
Barbet
Basset Artesien Normand
Basset Fauve De Bretagne
Basset Griffon VendÉen
Batard
Beauceron
Belgian Laekenois
Bergamasco
Berger De Picard
Black Russian Terrier
Black Forest Hound
Blackmouth Cur
Bleus de Gascogne
Bluetick Coonhound
Bolognese
Boykin Spaniel
Bracco Italiano
Braque d'AriÈge
Braque Bleu d'Auvergne
Braque du Bourbonnais
Braque Dupuy
Braque Saint-Germain
Braques FranÁais
Briquet Griffon Vendeen
Bruno De Jura
Cao da Serra De Aires
Cao de Castro Laboreiro
Cao de Fila Miguel
Canaan Dog
Canadian Eskimo Dog
Cane Corso
Carolina Dog
Catahoula Leopard Dog
Catalan Sheepdog

Caucasian Ovcharka
Central Asian Shepherd Dog
Central Asian Ovcharka
Cesky Terrier
Chart Polski
Chinese Foo Dog
Chinook
Cirneco dell'Etna
Coton De Tulear
Danish Broholmer
Dingo
Dogue De Bordeaux
Drentse Partridge Dog
Drever
Dutch Shepherd
English Coonhound
English Shepherd
English Toy Terrier
Entlebucher Sennenhund
Estrela Mountain Dog
Eurasier
Fauve De Bretagne
Fila Brasileiro
Finnish Lapphund
German Pinscher
German Spitz
Glen of Imaal Terrier
Grand-Anglo Francais
Greater Swiss Mountain
Greenland
Griffon Nivernais
G Basset Griffon Verdeen
G Basset Bleu Gascogne
Hamilton Hound
Havanese
Hanoverian Schweisshund
Hellenic Hound
Hokkaido Ken
Holland Shepherd
Hovawart
Iceland Sheepdog
Irish Red & White Setter
Jadgterrier
Japanese Spitz
Jindo
Kai Dog
Kangal Dog
Karelian Bear Dog
Karelo-Finnish Laika

Karst Shepherd
King Shepherd
Kishu
Kirhiz
Kooikerhondje
Kyi-Leo
Lagotto Romagnolo
Leonberger
Lowchen
Magyar Agar
Maremma Abbruzze
Middle Asian Ovtcharka
Mi-Ki™ Miniature Australian Shepherd
Min-Pei
Mountain Cur
Moscow Longhaired Toy Terrier
Mudi
Munsterlander
Neapolitan Mastiff
New Guinea Singing Dog
Norrbottenspets
North American Miniature Australian Shepherd
Norwegian Buhund
Norwegian Lundehund
Nova Scotia Duck Tolling Retriever
Ogar Polski
Old Danish Pointer
Olde English Bulldogge
Owczarek Podhalanski
Patterdale Terrier
Perdigueiro Portugueso
Portuguese Pointer
Perro De Agua
Peruvian Inca Orchid
Petit Bleu De Gascogne
Picardy Shepherd
Picardy Spaniel
Plott Hound
Podengo Canario
Podengo Pequeno
Poievin
Polish Tatra Sheepdog
Polski Owczarek Nizinny
Porcelaine
Portuguese Wirehaired

Podengo Medio
Pressa Mallorquin
Presa Canario
Pumi
Pyrenean Mastiff
Pyrenean Shepherd
Rastreador Brasileiro
Rat Terrier
Redbone Coonhound
Redtick Coonhound
Russian European Liaka
Sabuesos Espaóles
Sarplaninac
Schiller Hound
Segugio Italiano
Shiloh Shepherd
Sloughi
Slovensky Cuvac
Slovakian Hound
South Russian Steppe Hound
South Russian Ovtcharka
Spanish Mastiff
Spanish Waterdog
Spinone Italiano
Stabyhoun
Styrian Mountain
Swedish Vallhund
Teddy Roosevelt Terrier
Telomian
Tennessee Treeing Brindle
Terrier Brasileiro
Thai Ridgeback
Tibetan Kyi-Apso
Tibetan Mastiff
Tosa Inu
Transylvanian Hound
Treeing Walker Coonhound
Trigg Hound
Toy Fox Terrier
Tsvetnaya Bolonka
Tyrolean Hound
Volpino
Verelade
Wachtelhund
White Shepherd
Wirehair Styrian Mountain
Xoloitzcuintli (Standard-Toy)
Yugoslavian Hound

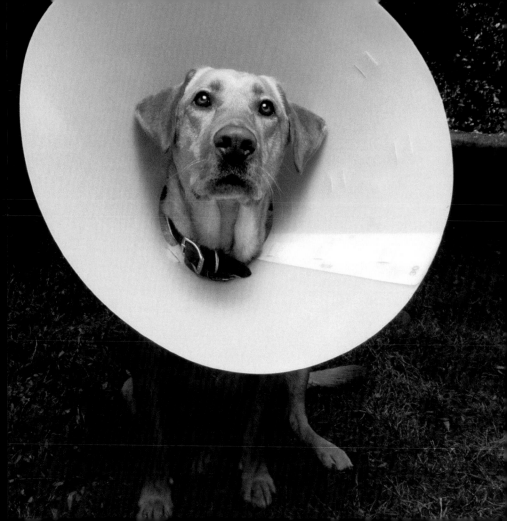

Worlds largest dog. The worlds heaviest as well as longest dog ever recorded was an Old English Mastiff named Zorba. In 1989, Zorba weighed 343lbs and was 8' 3" long from nose to tail! **World's tallest dog.** The tallest dog on record was named Shamgret Danzas. He was 42" tall and weighed 238 lbs. **World's smallest dog.** A tiny Yorkie from Blackburn, England. At two years of age and fully grown this little dude was an incredible 2.5" tall by 3.75" long! He weighed only 4 oz, approximately the size of a matchbox. **World's oldest dog.** An Australian cattle dog named Bluey. He was put to sleep at the age of 29 years and 5 months! **Best Drug Sniffing Dogs.** A U.S. Customs Labrador named "Snag" has made 118 drug seizures worth a canine record $810 million. The greatest number of drug seizures by dogs is 969 in 1988. IN ONE YEAR! The team of "Rocky" and "Barco" patrolled the Texas and Mexico border, alias "Cocaine Alley." They were so good that Mexican drug lords put a price of $30,000 on their heads. All dogs, from the **German Shepherd** to the tiny Poodle, are direct descendants of wolves. They can all breed together and produce fertile offspring. Technically they are of the same species. **Dogs can very easily regurgitate.** In fact, after eating wolves can travel significant distances back to their dens and regurgitate the food at will to feed their pups! **Dogs can see color** but it is not as vivid a color as we see. It is much like our vision at twilight. Some dogs have a **sense of smell** 1 million times greater than humans. **Canis Major:** The Great Dog—The great dog follows his master, Orion, as he makes his annual journey through

the sky. Sirius, also known as the **Dog Star**, is located on the shoulder of Canis Major. It is the brightest in the heavens, and its name means sparkling and scorching, as it is nearest to the sun during the height of summer. The hot, summer days: **Dog Days** — which Sirius was thought to cause, run from July 3rd to August 11th. The three stars of Orion's Belt point at the **Dog Star**, Sirius, in Canus major at Orion's heels. It is best seen in the northern hemisphere during winter, between December and March. Argos, or Argus, **Ulysses' hunting dog**, was the only creature to recognize the Greek hero when he returned home disguised as a beggar after 20 years of adventure. **Cerberus**, the three-headed dog of Greek mythology, guarded the gates to the underworld. **Laika** became the world's **first space traveler**. Russian scientists sent the small animal aloft in an artificial earth satellite in 1957. The basenji, an African wolf dog, is the **only dog that cannot bark**. Irish Wolfhounds rank as the **largest dog**, and Chihuahuas as the **smallest dog**. The St. Bernard is the **heaviest dog** and other breeds range in size between these extremes. A dog **can hear sounds 250 yards away** that most people cannot hear beyond 25 yards. The human ear can detect sound waves vibrating at frequencies up to 20,000 times a second, but dogs can hear sound waves that vibrate at frequencies of more than 30,000 times a second. Dogs have **twice as many** muscles for moving their ears as people. Dogs cannot see as well as humans and are considered **color blind**. A dog sees objects first by their movement, second by their brightness, and third by their shape. A dog's

heart beats between 70 and 120 times a minute, compared with a human heart which beats 70 to 80 times a minute. A **female** carries her young about 60 days before the puppies are born. Dogs (and wolves & foxes) are descended from a small, **weasel-like mammal** called Miacis which was a **tree-dwelling** creature and existed about 40 million years ago. Dogs, as we know them today, first appeared in Eurasia about 13,000 years ago, and were probably a direct descendant of a small, grey wolf (not from the type of jackal or **jackal/wolf** as previously thought). The **dingo** is not native to Australia but was introduced thousands of years ago by the first immigrants. Dogs were first domesticated by cavemen in the Paleolithic age and gradually developed (or were bred) into the breeds known today. The **tallest dogs** are the Great Dane and the Irish Wolfhound. The largest Great Dane stood at 41 inches and an Irish **Wolfhound** 39 inches. Dogs have been used as guards, hunters, draught animals, eyes for the blind, drug and explosive detectors, rodent controllers — and even weapons! In Roman times and the Middle Ages, mastiffs wearing light armor, **carrying spikes and pots of flaming sulphur and resin** ran into battle against mounted knights. In World War II the Russians trained dogs to run suicide missions between the tracks of German tanks with mines strapped on their backs. **Many foot disorders** in dogs are related to **long toenails**. Check your dog's nails once a month and trim when necessary, avoiding the vein. Sadly, statistics indicate that **eight million pets** lose their lives in animal shelters each year due to **overpopulation**. More than **five**

million puppies are born every year in the United States. In America, about one family in three owns a dog. The normal body temperature for a dog is **101.2 degrees** Fahrenheit. Though neutering has no effect on the overall personality, male dogs tend to display less aggression and **territorial behavior** when they are **neutered**. They are also less likely to contract urogenital diseases. If your dog has **bad breath**, he may need his teeth cleaned. The Boy Scouts, the Girl Scouts, and the 4-H Club all offer **merit badges** in dog care. **Dogs are pack animals** by nature. They need closeness, touching, and **petting** to be content and **happy**. Dogs are able to see much better in dim light than humans are. This is due to the tapetum lucidum, a light-reflecting layer behind the retina. Because it functions like a mirror, it also accounts for the **strange shine or glow** in a dog's eyes at night. The average dog's bite exerts 150 to 200 pounds of pressure per square inch. Some dogs can apply up to **450 pounds of pressure**. People have been keeping dogs as pets for the **past 12,000 years**. Dogs that are not around people before they reach the age of three months seldom turn out to be **good pets**. Puppies should remain with their mother until they are at least eight weeks old. Puppies **need to chew** to stimulate the loss of their baby teeth and to help place their permanent teeth. To a young puppy, **exercise and play** are the day's most important events. As a dog gets older, he **lives for dinnertime**. A dog needs to work off excess energy every day. Anyone can buy a dog, but it takes a kind owner to get its **tail wagging**. *(facts gathered from www.dogquotes.com)*

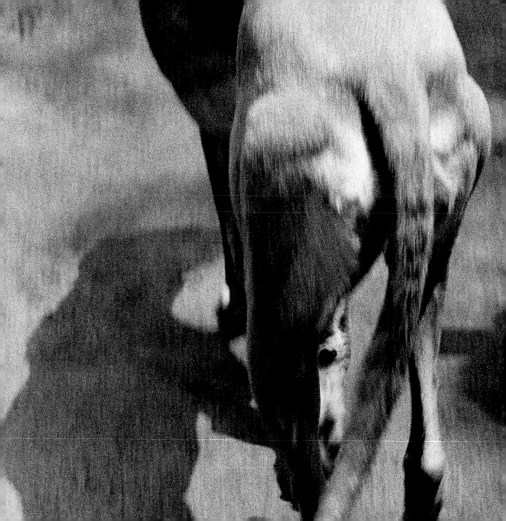

A man's best friend is his dog.

Dogs are really people with short legs in fur coats.

Family and friends welcome. Fleas are not.

If you want the best seat in the house...move the dog.

Life is just one table scrap after another.

My dog's not spoiled ... I'm just well trained.

Gone to the dogs.

Children are for people who can't have dogs.

A barking dog never bites.

Every dog has his day.

Barking up the wrong tree.

Wife and dog missing...$25 reward for dog.

Dog Star.

Let sleeping dogs lie.

Chasing your tail gets you nowhere...'cept back where you started.

Tail wagging the dog.

You can't teach an old dog new tricks.

Dog

bitch (f)

sire

(pl.) dogs

whelp (snd.)

(m) stud

group of = pack

I bought my grandmother a Seeing Eye dog. But he's a little sadistic. He does impressions of cars screeching to a halt.
—*Larry Amoros*

I like driving around with my two dogs, especially on the freeways. I make them wear little hats so I can use the car-pool lanes.
—*Monica Piper*

It was a small town: Ferguson, Ohio. When you entered there was a big sign and it said, "Welcome to Ferguson. Beware of the Dog." The all-night drugstore closed at noon.
—*Jackie Vernon*

When there is an old maid in the house, a watchdog is unnecessary.
—*Honore de Balzac. 1799-1850 French Novelist.*

Dumb dog. I bought a dog whistle. He won't use it.
—*Unknown*

A guy wanted the vet to cut his dog's tail off. The vet asked why. Well, my mother in law is visiting next month and I want to eliminate any possible indication that she is welcome.
—*Unknown*

Did you ever notice when you blow in a dog's face he gets mad at you? But when you take him in a car he sticks his head out the window!
—*Steve Bluestone*

Better not take a dog on the space shuttle, because if he sticks his head out when you're coming home his face might burn up.
—*"DEEP THOUGHTS" by Jack Handy*

Life is like a dogsled team. If you ain't the lead dog, the scenery never changes.
—*Lewis Grizzard*

There are three faithful friends— an old wife, an old dog and ready money.
—*Ben Franklin*

The other day I saw two dogs walk over to a parking meter. One says to the other, "How do you like that? Pay toilets!"
—*Dave Starr*

They say the dog is man's best friend. I don't believe that. How many of your friends have you neutered?
—*Larry Reeb*

I went to an exclusive kennel club. It was very exclusive.
There was a sign out front: "No Dogs Allowed."
—*Phil Foster*

He that lieth down with dogs, shall rise up with fleas.
—*Ben Franklin*

When you leave them in the morning, they stick their nose
in the door crack and stand there like a portrait until
you turn the key eight hours later.
—*Erma Bombeck*

I've been on so many blind dates I should get a free dog.
—*Wendy Liebman*
.
Oh, that dog! Ever hear of a German shepherd that
bites its nails? Barks with a lisp?
You say, "Attack!" And he has one. All he does is piddle.
He's nothing but a fur-covered kidney that barks.
—*Phillis Diller*

They have dog food now for constipated dogs. If your dog is
constipated, why screw up a good thing?
Stay indoors and let 'em bloat!
—*David Letterman*

If you want to be liked, get a dog.
The people you work with are not your friends.

—*Deborah Norville*

Dog Names: Aardvark, Abbott, Acorn, Adam, Agnew, Albuquerque, Alcoholic, AM, Amen, Amos, Armadillo, Aromatherapy, Arpeggio, Asterisk, Au Gratin, Au Revoir, Aubrey, Audrey, Auld Lang Sine, Austin, Awesome, Babble, Babushka, Babyface,

The greatest pleasure of a dog is that you may make a fool of yourself with him, and not only will he not scold you, but he will make a fool of himself, too.

—Samuel Butler

What counts is not necessarily the size of the dog in the fight; it's the size of the fight in the dog.

—*Dwight D. Eisenhower*

Big Red Pants Dog, Bill Clinton, Billabong, Billy Whiskers, Biscuit, Black Ice, Blackjack, Blacksheep, Blacky, Blah-blah, Blanket, Blitzen, Blonde Monica, Blondie, Bloody Mary, Blankity-blank, Blotto, Blubber, Bob Pin, Boilermaker, Boo-Boo,

Outside of a dog, a book is man's best friend.
Inside of a dog it's too dark to read.

—*Groucho Marx*

Boom-Boom, Boomerang, Boomhauer, Booty, Bosch, Bossa-nova, Bothersome, Bovine, Bozo, Brain, Bratwurst, Breakfast, Brie, Brine, Bruce, Bubkas, Buckminster, Buddha, Buddy, Buffalo Bill, Bug, Bugeye, Bullwinkle, Bumkin,

One reason the dog has so many friends:
He wags his tail instead of his tongue.

Unknown

Bumstead, Bunky, Burger, Burly, Bushwick, Butch, Butter, Buttercup, Buzzard, Buzzy, Caboodle, Caesar, Cagney, Calculator, Calder, Caldwell, Calico, Calzone, Canary, Capone, Captain Kirk, Captain Tweed, Caramel, Carl Perkins,

If you pick up a starving dog and make him prosperous, he will not bite you; that is the principal difference between a dog and a man.

—*Mark Twain*

Carpool, Cashmere, Castro, Cat Pee, Cauliflower, Caviar, CD-Rom, Cha-Cha, Chamber of Commerce, Chambermaid, Chaney, Chaos, Chaplin, Chapstick, Chapter 7, Chatty McFatty, Chaz, Ché, Checkers, Cheech, Cheerios, Cheese,

**Here, Gentlemen,
a dog teaches us a lesson in humanity.**

—Napoleon Bonaparte

Cheese Puff, Cheeto, Chein, Chekhov, Chewy, Cheyenne, Chicken Joe, Chicky, Chigger, Chinchilla, Chinook, Chipmunk, Chipper, Chips, Chong, Choo-Choo Valdez, Chopsticks, Chorizo, Chowder, Chroma, Chub, Chubbiest, Chubblette,

**To his dog, every man is Napoleon;
hence the constant popularity of dogs.**

—Aldous Leonard Huxley

Chubfish, Chuck D, Chupacabra, Chuppa-Chup, City Hall, Clancy, Clarence, Clay, Claws, Cleitus, Cleo, Clorox, Cluck,
Clueless, Clyde, Cockroach, Cocopuff, Coffee Bean, Columbo, Condor, Conga, Conway Twitty, Coondog, Corduroy, Corky,

You can say any foolish thing to a dog, and the dog will give you a look that says, 'My God, you're right! I never would've thought of that!'

—*Dave Barry*

Corn Dog, Corn Pone, Cornelius, Cosmo, Couch, Courvoisier, Cousin, Cowboy, Cracker Jack, Crash, Crayon, Cream Puff, Crescendo, Critter, Croissant, Crouton, Crumb, Crunch, Cuddles, Cuervo, Cupcake, Cupid, Cyber, Czar, Czech, Dacron,

I love a dog. He does nothing for political reasons.

—*Will Rogers*

Dafoe, Dagwood, Dali, Dandelion, Dang-Bang-Shang-a-Lang-Fang-Rang-Tang, Daredevil, Darling, Data, Daze, Dead Kenny, Dead Meat, Deadwood Dick, Deimos, Deja Vu, Delicious, DeMille, Demitri, Denim, Derek, Dice, Dick Dale, Dick

**Man is an animal that makes bargains;
no other animal does this.
One dog does not change a bone with another.**

—Adam Smith

**If your dog doesn't like someone
you probably shouldn't either.**

—Unknown

Echo, Eggman, El Camino, Eli, Elliot, Elwood, Ergo, Eskimo, Exit, Fancy, Fandango, Farts, Fatty, Fear, Feet, Fez, Fickle, Filibuster, Fingerprint, Flea, Float, Fluffer-Nutter, FM, Forgetaboutit, Fork, Fox-trot, Fragment, Frampton, Fresco, Frisky,

Even a dog distinguishes between stumbled over and being kicked.

—*Oliver Wendell Holmes Jr.*

Frito, Frodo, Frog, Fruit Juice, Fudgy, Funk, Funyon, Fusion, Fuzzy Dice, Garbo, George Stephanopoulos, Gibberish, Gnoocchi, Goathead, God, Godiva, Gouache, Goulash, Goya, Green Chile, Grover, Grubb, Grunt, Gustav, Hablaba,

If you get to thinkin' you're a person of some influence, try orderin' somebody else's dog around.

—Cowboy wisdom

Hairy Truman, Happy Camper, Happy Hour, Hawk Food, Hawkeye, Hector, Hello, Hello Kitty, Helper Monkey, Helvetica, Hero, Hieronymus, Hippodamus, Hoagie, Homer, Homophone, Hoopla, Hops, Hot Toddy, Houdini, Housewife, Hula-

In dog years, I'm dead.

—*Unknown*

hoop, Humpty Dumpty, Ink Pen, Jack Kerouac, Jack Ruby, Jack-in-the-Box, Jean Cocteau, Jelly Roll, Jimmy Carter, Jitterbug, Job, Joe Six-pack, John Connor, Judge Judy, Julius, Jupiter, Kafka, Kahlua, Kandinsky, Keely, Keith, Ketchup,

The more people I meet the more I like my dog.

—Unknown

Kilo, King Kong, Kiwi, Klepto, Klezmer, Klimt, Kudos, Kumquat, Kurt, Lady, Latte, Lautrec, Lazy Bones, Lee Harvey Oswald, Leon, Les Nessman, Lexan, Lexicon, Little Lord Font LeRoy, Little Orphan Annie, Little Red Riding Hood, Loaf,

If dogs could talk it would take a lot of the fun out of owning one.

—Andy Rooney

Lock Jaw, Logic, Lovey, Low Rider, Lucky, Lumpin', Lumpy, Macher, Macho, Mackin', Mackinaw, Mad Hatter, Madam Chairperson, Magic, Magilla Gorilla, Malcolm X, Mao, Marky Mark, Martha Stewart, Mary Worth, Master, Matisse,

**[Dogs] never talk about themselves
but listen to you while you talk about yourself,
and keep up an appearance of
being interested in the conversation.**

—Jerome K. Jerome

Maximummer, Maya, Mazzaroth, MC 900 ft. dog, MC Anything, McFatty, Meadow, Meatloaf, Mecca, Medusa, Memo, Mentsh, Merle, Michiana, Microfiche, Mike D, Mimosa, Ming, Mini-me, Missy, Mitosis, Momento, Mona Lisa, Monophonic,

When a dog wags her tail and barks at the same time, how do you know which end to believe?

—*Anonymous*

If you eliminate smoking and gambling, you will be amazed to find that almost all an Englishman's pleasures can be, and mostly are, shared by his dog.

—*George Bernard Shaw*

Things that upset a terrier may pass virtually unnoticed by a Great Dane.

—Smiley Blanton

**I've seen a look in dogs' eyes,
a quickly vanishing look of amazed contempt,
and I am convinced that basically
dogs think humans are nuts.**

—John Steinbeck

Raspberry, Ravioli, Rayon, Refusenik, Relax, Reservoir Dog, Retarded, Retarding, Richarding, Robin Hood, Rockefeller, Rocket Dog, Rococo, Romulan, Rooster, Rosa Luxemburg, Salinger, Salt Peanuts, Santa Claws, Scanter, Scenster,

**Dogs are getting bigger,
according to a leading dog manufacturer.**

—Leo Rosten

Schmattah, Schmeel, Schmutz, Schubert, Scott Joplin, Scotty, Scrap Paper, Scrappy, Scruffs, Scruffy, Senseless, Sentence, Sfumato, Shadrak, Shaggs, Shakes, Shamrock, Shlitz, Shortcake, Sir, Sirius, Skids, Skinny Puppy, Skyrocket,

If a picture wasn't going very well
I'd put a puppy dog in it,
always a mongrel, you know,
never one of the full bred puppies.
And then I'd put a bandage on its foot...
I like it when I did it, but now I'm sick of it.

—*Norman Rockwell.*

**Did you ever walk into a room
and forget why you walked in?
I think that is how dogs spend their lives.**

—Sue Murphy

**I named my dog 'Stay'...
so I can say 'Come here, Stay. Come here, Stay.'**

—Steven Wright

The Good One, The Goof, Thor, Thorax, Thoreau, Tibbets, Tigger, Tippy, Tips, Titmouse, Todd, Too-Short, Topical Lotion, Topsy, Toulouse, Trick, Trinity, Trompe L'Oeil, Trotsky, Tuna Fish, Turkey, Turnip, Tuxedo, Twickenham, Twink, Twinkie, Two

All knowledge, the totality of all questions and all answers is contained in the dog.

—Franz Kafka

Chewbaccas, Tyrone, Ulysses, Umbrella, Umbria, Underdog, Unique, Use Other Dog, Useless, Utopia, Van Gogh, Vanderbilt, Vanilla, Verdi, Virginia Wolfe, VISA, Vitruvius, Vodka, Volkswaggon, Vonnegut, Wade, Waffles, Wanted, Weasel,

**Dogs feel very strongly that they
should always go with you in the car,
in case the need should arise for them to bark
violently at nothing right in your ear.**

—Dave Barry.

Wally, Whippets, Wife, Whistler, Wiggles, William Blake, Willie Wonka, Wimpy, Wizard of Oz, Wompit, Y2K, Yak, Yentle, Yellow, Yiddisher Kop, Yippie, Yogurt, York, You're Ugly, Zero, Zilch, Zine, Zippy, Zit Cream, Zoo, Zorba, Zuzax

If a dog's prayer were answered, bones would rain from the sky.

—*Old proverb*

Names for two dogs: AC & DC, Adam & Eve, Amos & Andy, Anthony & Cleopatra, Astair & Rodgers, Aurora & Borealis, Babe & Ruth, Bart & Homer, Barbie & Ken, Ben & Jerry, Bill & Hillary, Biscuit & Gravy, Boggie & Woggie,

No one appreciates the very special genius of your conversation as the dog does.

—Christopher Morley

Bold & Italic, Burns & Allen, Captain & Tenille, Cat & Mouse, Checks & Balances, Chip & Dale, Click & Clack, Corn & Cobb, Country & Western, Cracker & Jack, Crispy & Crunchy, Debit & Credit, Dick & Jane, Dick & Tracy, Donny & Marie,

My dog is worried about the economy because Alpo is up to 99 cents a can. That's almost $7 in dog money.

—Joe Weinstein

Yesterday I was a dog.
Today I'm a dog.
Tomorrow I'll probably still be a dog.
Sigh! There's so little hope for advancement.

—Snoopy

Oh, yeah, what are you gonna do?
Release the dogs? Or the bees?
Or the dogs with bees in their mouths
and when they bark,
they shoot bees at you?

—*Homer Simpson*

**How many legs does a dog have
if you call the tail a leg?
Four.
Calling a tail a leg doesn't make it a leg.**

—Abraham Lincoln

"How's it going Mr. Peterson?"
"It's a dog eat dog world, Woody,
and I'm wearing milk bone underwear."

—*Norm from Cheers*

& Dazzle, Ritz & Cracker, Robo & Cop, Rocky & Bullwinkle, Rogers & Hammerstein, Romeo & Juliet, Rosemary & Thyme, Rum & Coke, Salt & Pepper, Simon & Garfunkel, Sourcream & Onions, Spock & Kirk, Starsky & Hutch, Sticks &

[My dog] can bark like a congressman, fetch like an aide, beg like a press secretary, and play dead like a receptionist when the phone rings.

—Gerald B. H. Solomon, U.S. Congressman
(Entry in contest to identify Capitol Hill's Great American Dog. New York Times, August 9, 1986.)

Stones, Sonny & Cher, Sweet & Sour, Thelma & Louise, Thick & Thin, Tiffany & Cartier, Tigger & Pooh, Toast & Jelly, Turner & Hooch, Trick & Treat, Tutti & Frutti, Up & Down, Under & Over, Venus & Pluto, Worm & Toad, Wilma & Betty, Yankee

He's fair. He treats us all the same — like dogs.

—Henry Jordan, Green Bay Packers right tackle, on Vince Lombardi, recalled on Lombardi's death. September 3, 1970.

& Doodle, Yarn & Thread, Zig & Zag. **Three Dogs**: 1 & 2 & 3, A & B & C, Alpha & Omega & Delta, Alvin & Simon & Theodore, April & May & June, Archie & Veronica & Jughead, Aster & Rose & Daisy, And & Is & If, Bart & Lisa & Maggie,

A dog is the only thing on earth that loves you more than you love yourself.

—Josh Billings

Cindy & Jan & Marsha, Curly & Larry & Mo, Doug & Skeeter & Patti, Earth & Wind & Fire, Enchilada & Burrito & Taco, Faith & Hope & Charity, Giles & Giles & Fripp, Godel & Escher & Bach, Going & And Going & And Gone, Greg, Peter & Bobby,

**When a man's best friend is his dog,
that dog has a problem.**

—Edward Abbey

Huey & Lewy & Dewey, Huey & Lewis & The News, Mary & Kate & Ashley, Nick & Nack & Pattywack, NBC & CBS & ABC,
Peanut & Butter & Jelly, Porkroll & Egg & Cheese, Rain & Sleet & Snow, Red & Green & Blue, Rose & Violet & Lily, Rub

**The average dog is a nicer person
than the average person.**

—Andy Rooney

& A Dub & Dub, Science & Math & Social Studies, Shadrack & Meshack & Bednago, Sink & Sank & Sunk, Sun & Moon & Stars, Spam & Nuttella & Oreo, Spanky & Alfalfa & Darla, Spring & Winter & Autumn, The Butcher & The Baker & The

When a dog bites a man that is not news, but when a man bites a dog that is news.

—Charles Anderson Dana, 'What Is News?'
The New York Sun, 1882

Candlestick Maker, Tom & Dick & Harry, Tic & Tac & Toe, Twilight & Moonlight & Dawn, Walker & Texas & Ranger. **Four Dogs**: Crispy, Crunchy, Big & Fatty,   Cyan, Magenta, Yellow & Black,   Juicy, Tender, Flavorful & Cuts, Four, Score, Seven

**My dog is half pit bull, half poodle.
Not much of a watchdog, but a vicious gossip!**

—Craig Shoemaker

& Years Ago, GQ, Style, Vouge & Mademoiselle, Here, There, Every & Where, Perch, Trout, Blue Gill & Bass, Pen, Pencil, Paperclip & Ruler, Richer, Poorer, Better & Worse, Up, Down, Under & Over, Zero, Ziltch, Nada & Nothing.

Don't accept your dog's admiration as conclusive evidence that you are wonderful. Ann Landers

Three things it is best to avoid: a strange dog, a flood, and a man who thinks he is wise. Welsh proverb

The dog wags his tail, not for you, but for your bread. Portuguese proverb

The barking of a dog does not disturb the man on a camel. Egyptian proverb

Children aren't dogs; adults aren't gods. Haitian proverb

Beware of a silent dog and still water. Latin proverb

One dog barks at something; the rest bark at him. Chinese proverb

Do not respond to a barking dog. Moroccan saying

Only mad dogs and Englishmen go out in the noonday sun. Indian proverb

Those who sleep with dogs will rise with fleas.
Italian proverb

Show a dog a finger, and he wants the whole hand.
Yiddish proverb

**If you are a host to your guest, be a host
to his dogs also.** Russian proverb

**A house without a cat or a dog is the house
of a scoundrel.** Portuguese proverb

**An honest man is not the worse because
a dog barks at him.** Danish proverb

Every dog is allowed one bite. Common law proverb

A good dog deserves a good bone. U.S. proverb

**If you stop every time a dog barks, your road
will never end.** Saudi Arabian saying